THE RIGHT TO CHOOSE
Questions of Feminist Morality

by

Ruth Riddick

RUTH RIDDICK has worked with the Irish Family Planning Association, the Dublin Well Woman Centre and the Irish Pregnancy Counselling Centre. In 1983, at the height of the Eighth Amendment Referendum campaign, she set up Open Line Counselling, a non-directive pregnancy counselling service. She administered Open Line until its closure in 1987, following a High Court injunction which is currently under consideration by the European Court of Human Rights. Most recently, she has worked as Administrator of Foyle Film Projects and also works as a freelance journalist.

© Ruth Riddick

First published in 1990 by
Attic Press,
44 East Essex Street,
Dublin 2.

British Library Cataloguing in Publication Data
Riddick, Ruth
    The right to choose : questions of feminist morality. -
    (LIP pamphlets.)
    1. Abortion. Ethical aspects.
    I. Title II. Series
    179.76

    ISBN 0-946211-85-X

Cover Design: Paula Nolan
Typesetting: Attic Press
Printing: Elo Press

This is for Isabelle Shaw

ACKNOWLEDGEMENTS

I would like to thank the following friends and colleagues for their ideas, support and companionship throughout the development of this pamphlet:

Sherie de Burgh, Clodagh Corcoran, Christine Donaghy, Brendan Ellis, Christine Falls, Colin Francome, Paul de Grae, Germaine Greer, Susan Himmelweit, Attracta Ingram, Frances Kissling, Diane Munday, Anne O'Neill, Rosalind Pollack Petchesky, Kevin Rockett, Corrina Reynolds, Madeleine Simms, Attic Press, Dee Sullivan, clients and staff of the Irish Pregnancy Counselling Centre and Open Line Counselling, and especially Fiacc O Brolchain.

PREFACE

Sometime in the last ten years, I had the experience of counselling a working-class Belfast woman with a crisis pregnancy. We met in the inauspicious surroundings of the Central railway station. At 22 years of age, she was already the glorious widow of a republican martyr. She was Roman Catholic, abortion is murder and she was not to be permitted in her widowhood to have a sexual relationship, much less to produce incontrovertible evidence of her 'betrayal'. This unlovely story is but one from the largely unwritten and unspoken annals of the Irish abortion reality, north and south.

I was reminded of this incident, one of thousands I've encountered as Director of a non-directive pregnancy counselling service, when I was invited to review the published findings of an international enquiry into abortion in northern Ireland. It occurred to me that there is no such contemporary statement on the situation in the Republic, despite the momentous political and legal developments of the eighties.

A further spur to reopening the right to choose debate came from the experience of being a panel member on RTE's *Questions & Answers* programme during which a self-satisfied Fianna Fáil politician assured me and our viewers that 'these matters' had been dealt with once and for all by the Human Life Amendment of 1983 - this in a jurisdiction which daily exports ten abortion cases to England, amendments, court orders and injunctions notwithstanding.

Abortion is an issue on which it is possible to have only one public stand in Ireland - unequivocal opposition. This naturally produces a situation in which individual women's voices are silenced, to be replaced by faceless abortion statistics. In the twenty-three years of the British Abortion Act only three Irish women have publicly named themselves as women who have had abortions. In this silence, in these statistics, real women live - individuals, citizens, decision-makers, moral agents.

I have written this pamphlet as an intervention into that silence. It is not, however, the purpose of this pamphlet to make the case for 'allowing' women to have abortions under certain preconditions, nor will I argue for the introduction of legislation permitting abortion (although many will see this as an inevitable implication). Similarly, I have discussed Irish women's abortion experience elsewhere and will not repeat myself here. My project is rather to argue that women are moral agents, that their abortion decisions may be moral decisions. Abortion, as the ultimate exercise of individual fertility control, is the arena in which women have least social acknowledgment and support; it is, therefore, the context in which women's right to choose, that is, women's right to act as moral agents, must be argued.

Of necessity, the discussion here will be introductory. However, debate on these issues has been too long silenced. It is time to reopen Pandora's Box.

Ruth Riddick

PROLOGUE
CHOICE IN CONTEMPORARY IRELAND

We are continuing to ignore the real needs and the real problems of our society and continuing to close down the possibility of access to advice and help. I have no doubt at all that the abortion figures will rise strikingly over the years and it is our direct responsibility and particularly the responsibility of Irish politicians.

Mary Robinson, 1980

In late 1979, a small group of Irish feminists proclaimed themselves the 'Women's Right to Choose Group'. The principal aims of the group were the decriminalisation of abortion, illegal under the 1861 Offences Against the Person Act, and the establishment of a feminist pregnancy counselling service for women in crisis. This latter aim was almost immediately achieved with the opening, in June 1980 and under the Group's management, of the Irish Pregnancy Counselling Centre. As early as March of that year, the Women's Right to Choose Group hosted a public meeting in Liberty Hall, Dublin. The platform included journalists Jill Tweedie from Britain and Mary Holland, together with representatives from the Group itself and from the Irish Pregnancy Counselling Centre. Chairing the meeting was Professor Mary McAleese, then a well-known broadcaster, who later claimed to have misunderstood the nature of the meeting. The attendance was vocally antagonistic and the atmosphere highly charged. As an ordinary member of the public, I addressed the meeting from the back of the hall. The *Evening Herald* (11 March 1981) reported:

> A woman, who admitted having an abortion, spoke out strongly in favour of a woman's right to control her own body last night. Ruth Riddick said that the men of this country are not enlightened enough, or chose not to be, when it comes to the question of taking positive steps to avoid pregnancy. They have a right to choose whether they will take responsibility for their actions or not. So why should the basic right of control of one's body be denied to women, she asked.

This unplanned intervention was to have far-reaching consequences for me. I was offered an administrative position with the Irish Pregnancy Counselling Centre and it was through this involvement that I came to realise just how significant the question of fertility control is to women's everyday lives. I also came to see the political importance of offering woman-to-woman help, a 'self-help' process which the women's movement had developed in the 1970s in such groups and campaigns as the Rape Crisis Centres and Women's Aid. This importance is (if possible) magnified where questions of fertility are at stake - the right of women to reject compulsory motherhood is not popular in our society.

Meanwhile, the backlash against a perceived liberalisation of Irish society was under way. Right-wing moralists, quite independently of the existence of the Women's Right To Choose Group, had already focussed on abortion as the issue around which they would 'halt the permissive tide in other areas' (John O'Reilly, *Need for a Human Life Amendment*, January 1981). The foundations of a right-to-life movement had been laid in the 1970s and it only remained for a highly organised 'Pro-Life' Amendment Campaign to convince the legislature of the urgency of its cause.

The Campaign took as its model the American 'Human Life Amendment Campaign', which had been launched in the 1970s and which remains a live issue today. The Eighth Amendment campaign of 1982/3, as it became, was to prove long, bitter and divisive, undermining even friendships of long-standing.

During this campaign, the Women's Right To Choose Group suffered a number of body blows: the group split internally; the official opposition to the amendment, known simply as the 'Anti-Amendment Campaign', distanced itself from 'The Right to Choose'; and, finally, the Irish Pregnancy Counselling Centre collapsed under financial pressure, to be replaced, in July 1983, at the height of the Amendment Campaign, by Open Line Counselling . My decision to establish this service was taken for professional, political and personal reasons; specifically, my colleagues and I would not abandon our (future) clients, nor would we allow our service to be intimidated by the anti-choice lobby.

On 7 September 1983, 53% of the electorate, went to the polls to decide the issue of the Eighth Amendment: 66.45% of those who voted agreed to its adoption. Consequently, this provision became Article 40.3.3 of the Irish Constitution. It reads:

> The State acknowledges the right to life of the unborn and, with due regard to the equal right to life of the mother, guarantees in its laws to respect, and as far as practicable, by its laws to defend and vindicate that right.

The 'right-to-life' victory was to have serious consequences for the Women's Movement. Not only was a fundamental feminist demand overwhelmingly rejected at the polls but many sections of the Women's Movement and the Left had already abandoned the campaign for abortion rights. The issue was dropped from the media and both the Women's Right to Choose Group and the break-away Right to Choose Campaign eventually disbanded. The focus of subsequent debate became the *practical* right of access to information about (lawful) abortion services abroad, as, on foot of the Amendment, the anti-choice movement succeeded through the courts in suspending the formal provision of non-directive pregnancy counselling. The contemporary successor to the Women's Right To Choose Group is known as the 'Women's Information Network' and operates independently of the (former) pregnancy counselling services. A consideration of women's *moral* right to choose has been virtually abandoned.

Speaking on the first anniversary of the amendment, the President of the Society for the Protection of the Unborn Child (SPUC) issued the following challenge:

> In order to defend the right to life of the unborn, we must close the *abortion referral agencies* which are operating in Dublin quite openly and underneath the eyes of the law. These clinics must be closed and if the 1861 Act cannot close them, we must have another Act that will. (emphases mine).

The non-directive pregnancy counselling services (Open Line Counselling and the Dublin Well Woman Centre, a women's health facility) were thus targeted as the anti-choice movement succeeded in achieving a High Court order (known colloquially as 'the Hamilton judgement') closing the service. *The Irish Times* of the day commented:

> With just four days to go to closure, Kate says it's been like Heuston Station ... I sit in the adjoining waiting room with her client's sister, Elaine. Looking up from her magazine, Elaine says she first heard about Open Line's counselling service through a friend who had been there. So she took her pregnant sister Ann up on the bus from Mayo that morning. They could have come from Tullamore, Tuam, Donegal or Dingle ... Elaine says she hasn't heard anything about Open Line closing down on January 12, the day the High Court order comes into effect. Indeed, little did Elaine know that Open Line had already ordered the removal van.
>
> Lorna Siggins, *The Irish Times*, 9 January 1987

Having been, in a colleague's memorable phrase, 'made constitutionally redundant', we established an emergency telephone network, the first of its kind in the country, offering access to (anonymous) professional pregnancy counsellors and to information on lawful abortion services abroad. Callers to the Helpline, co-ordinated through my personal telephone, increasingly emphasised information, rather than counselling, as their priority - that is, information about reputable abortion services in the UK. While the women and the many men who call do appreciate the opportunity of discussing their crisis pregnancy, the valuable role which counselling can play in the decision-making process has been grievously undermined by the separation of 'information' from 'counselling', the effect of the Supreme Court Order of March 1988 (where our Appeal against the Order of the High Court failed). The Chief Justice, Mr Thomas A Finlay was unambiguous:

> There could not be an implied and unenumerated constitutional right to information about the availability of a service of abortion outside the State which, if availed of, would have the direct consequence of destroying the expressly guaranteed right to life of the unborn.
>
> *Supreme Court Record* 185/87, 16 March 1988

It seems to me that this judgement was indeed the only course of action open to the Courts, in the light of Article 40.3.3, and for the following reasons

* the Court could not ban outright the practice of non-directive counselling without undermining the entire therapeutic services, a situation which would clearly not be in the public interest; therefore
* by disbarring certain organisations and individuals from disseminating information about abortion services legally obtainable abroad, the Court could be seen to uphold the rights guaranteed to the unborn, while being mindful that such an Order would be almost impossible to enforce and that women needing abortion would get the information anyhow. As the Chief Justice remarked: 'nor does the Order ... in any way prevent a pregnant woman from becoming aware of the existence of abortion outside the jurisdiction.'
>
> *Supreme Court Record* 185/87, 16 March 1988

That this judgement, for all its sophistry, fails to address either the social rights of women or the political demands of the anti-choice lobby has been borne out by recent developments, as evidenced by:

* the numbers of Irish women achieving lawful abortion in England remain virtually unchanged (allowing for slight annual variations);

* the number of cases currently and potentially before the Attorney General and the Courts seeking to impose a blanket ban on the dissemination of abortion information, a clearly unrealistic aim, given that this information is already in the public domain.

Just how long this information remains accessible is, however, otherwise uncertain, as the case of the monthly glossy magazine for women, *Cosmopolitan*, which has traditionally been marketed as a 'trendy' or 'quasi feminist' publication, illustrates. Page 171 of the January 1990 edition carries a Publisher's Note which reads:

Following complaints from the Office of Censorship of Publications in Dublin, this page, which is usually devoted to advertisements providing abortion advice and help, has been left blank in all editions of this magazine published for distribution in the Republic of Ireland. We deeply regret that we are unable to provide the relevant information, but we are advised that if we continue to publish these advertisements it could result in this magazine being made the subject of a Prohibition Order under the Censorship of Publications Act 1946 as amended by the Health (Family Planning) Act 1979.

Meanwhile, little is known or discussed about the actual experience of individual Irish women. Respondents to a questionnaire compiled in the UK by Open Line Counselling commented:

It would be so much easier if we could find out more about what goes on in London before we come over here. The decision to have an abortion is not half as difficult as trying to find out about clinics here.

Some Characteristics of Irish Women Seeking Abortion Services in Britain, January 1988

This is the real-life context in which the issues raised in this pamphlet are addressed.

ABORTION AND THE FEMINIST AGENDA

The history of abortion forms a continuous and irrefutable record of women's determination to make reproductive choices based on their own perceptions and definitions of their social, sexual and economic needs.

K Kaufmann, 1984

Abortion has been on the feminist agenda from the beginning. In 1967, the first conference of the American National Organisation of

Women was held in Washington, DC. The conference marked the formal beginning of the current wave of international feminism. Article VIII of the NOW Bill of Rights proclaims: 'The Right of Women to Control their Reproductive Lives', and includes on its list of demands: 'The right of women to control their own reproductive lives by ... repealing penal laws governing abortion.'

Only women have wombs; only women give birth. This single elemental fact assures that pregnancy is a uniquely female experience. For this reason, matters of the womb, questions of reproduction are central concerns of feminism.

Throughout much of recorded history and in most observed cultures, women are not only differentiated from men because of their womb and its powers, but are relegated to a private sphere where the privileges and power accorded males in the public world are denied them. This is clearly an issue for feminism.

Women, almost universally, are deemed to be at the mercy of their biology, that is, of the womb. Thus, the proposition that biology is destiny, a proposition which is refuted by feminism. So deep is the identification of woman and womb that psychoanalyst Eric Erikson can claim that, as Susan Moller Okin reports in her critique:

> The little girl develops around the possession of an 'inner space' with great potential - the womb. Woman's capacity to bear and nurse children is therefore not just one aspect of her nature; her entire identity and the life she lives must revolve around her 'inner space' and its desire to be filled.
> *Women in Western Political Thought*, 1979

Erikson himself is further quoted as saying 'Woman is nurturance ... anatomy decrees the life of a woman', an almost mythic siting of woman's very essence in the womb. Schools of medicine prescribe ever more radical invasions of the womb - caesarian sections, ovariectomy, hysterectomy - as a panacea for perceived manifestations of female pathology: ie vaginal birthing, the onset of menopause, even psychological/psychiatric disturbances. Even women's expression of rage and frustration, essentially intellectual responses to an objectively hostile world, are dismissed after the womb as hysteria.

A further question for feminists concerns the status of women in the social reality in which we live; are we 'girls', 'wives', 'mothers', 'citizens', 'persons', or none of these?

Under patriarchy, 'the rule of the fathers' in Mary Daly's phrase, the world is defined by, for and about men. Insofar as women are acknowledged in this world-view, it is as relatives - in our roles relative to men, as, for example, sex objects, the mother of 'my' children, 'my' wife etc. The family is a patriarchal unit with 'father' at its pinnacle and other family members defined by their relation to him - as wife, daughter, son. (The death of an individual father doesn't change these relations; we casually refer to 'his widow'.)

This proprietorial patriarchal relationship is clearly signalled in our society where women adopt by way of identification the surnames of their husbands and fathers.The primary social identification of women, then, is not in ourselves, nor as 'persons' or 'citizens', but in our relation to the patriarch. This means that the first right we must assert for ourselves is the identity of personhood, not simply in a spurious equality with men but as an elemental involvement in the world of morality, decision-making, responsibility, social accountability.

The degree of moral autonomy, personal choice and social responsibility afforded individuals will depend on whether they are considered to be 'persons' or 'relatives'. Women, as we have seen, are more generally assigned to relative status, a position clearly endorsed in Bunreacht na hEireann (the Constitution of the Republic of Ireland), the fundamental code of Irish law and social aspiration, adopted as recently as 1937. The Constitution makes only three specific references to women:

> The State acknowledges the right to life of the unborn and, with due regard to the equal right to life of the *mother*, guarantees in its laws to respect, and, as far as practicable, by its laws to defend and vindicate that right. (Article 40.3.3, 8th Amendment, adopted 7 September 1983)

> In particular, the State recognises that *by her life within the home*, woman gives to the State a support without which the common good cannot be achieved. (Article 41.2.1)

> The State shall, therefore, endeavour to ensure that *mothers* shall not be obliged by economic necessity to engage in labour to the neglect of their *duties in the home*. (Article 41.2.2)
> (italics mine)

Women in the Irish Constitution are 'mothers' with 'lives' and 'duties in the home'.

Article 40.3.3, the Eighth Amendment to the Constitution, was achieved in part through the exploitative use of pictures of babies to visually represent foetal life in utero. During the Amendment campaign, and subsequently, it was claimed that the womb, that most precious signifier of a woman, was no less than 'the most dangerous place in the world to be' - this in a world with the nuclear capacity to annihilate all life many times over.

These issues are of crucial concern to feminists in the light of an extraordinary late 20th century development - the legal idea of personhood of the foetus, the inhabitor and potential product of the womb. This new 'person', the foetus, qualifies for constitutional guarantees not necessarily extended to adult women and may constitute a litigant against women in matters of pre-natal care and birthing procedures.

Feminists are, then, by definition, concerned about matters of the womb and its powers for the following reasons:

* while the womb and its powers are elementally female (at once a site of deep pleasure and satisfaction for women, and a means and justification for exploitation and subjugation), women are more than the sum of womb and reproduction in the same way that men are more than the sum of penis and scrotum
* for women, the unique privilege of being female is perversely a means of reduction to the status of the womb's potential; of subjection to a reproductive capacity beyond our effective control - psychically, socially, philosophically, that is, of subjection to compulsory motherhood.

In short, biology is, or it is not, destiny; the question is ultimately not behavioural, nor technological, but moral.

In the light of these developments, and given the failure of the law, the medical profession, of moral philosophy itself, to clarify the procedure in cases of conflict between mother and foetus, the status of women is vital to our very survival (no idle concern, as the fate of Sheila Hodgers, whose post-partum death was caused by a non-uterine cancer aggravated by but 'morally' untreatable because of pregnancy, demonstrates. Ironically, this unnecessary death took place during the 'right to life' campaign in 1983).

If women are to be simply vessels for progeny - and there is clear evidence that the majority of male, mainstream philosophers and moral commentators, not to mention civil law makers, incline toward this view - how are women to prevail and how are we to defend ourselves against the (proposed) superior claims of the foetus in the (natural) womb?

Clearly these matters are of central concern to the feminist agenda.

THE CONCEPT OF INDIVIDUAL CHOICE

I would see the failure to provide abortion as a human rights issue.
Mary McAleese, 1980

Modern theories of political liberty and individual rights, evolving through 17th and 18th century social and moral philosophy, became popular through a series of political upheavals which were to have enormous consequences for our way of life - the English, American and French Revolutions, the last now merely two hundred years old, with its famous rallying cry of 'liberté, égalité, *fraternité'* (sic). Political debate in the western democracies has since been preoccupied with how individual rights may be justly balanced and incorporated into the larger political framework we call society, the State, or even 'the common good'.

One of the immediate difficulties raised by this political tradition is the question of whether a society committed to political liberty must also embrace women as holders of personal rights. While modern commentators suggest that such an embrace is implicit in codes such as, for example, Bunreacht na hEireann, a closer examination of both theory and practice would suggest to the contrary that the masculine terminology employed means just that - for men only. Political liberty, as envisaged by the founding 'fathers' of democracy, is for men only - women are to continue in their traditional ('natural') roles as relatives/servants. (This restriction on political liberty extends to other 'minorities', as in the case of our travelling people or in racist societies - hence the close identification by generations of white American feminists with the black movement for civil rights.)

One of the fundamental demands of feminism has always been and remains that women be acknowledged as persons with social and political rights; that is, included in and heirs to the tradition of political liberty. The specific rights which feminism claims for women belong firmly to that tradition.

Thus, the proposition that women have the right to choose presupposes that:

* women are heirs to the tradition of political liberty;
* women are persons of moral autonomy.

Western democracy, the political system which developed out of the social revolutions of the Enlightenment, endeavours, albeit with some discomfort, to balance a number of (seemingly) discordant demands, such as:

* the interests of the nation-state
* the interests of international capital
* the demands of the common good
* the rights of minority interests.

Some of these demands may be inherently exclusive; the modern economic trend, for example, favours a monetary internationalism (as in the projected EC single market) over national economies. (This economic philosophy was challenged in Ireland during the referendum to decide ratification of the Single European Act. Opponents of the SEA included not only individualist economists but the Left and the 'right to life' movement, a bizarre coalition.) Similarly the common good is often pitted against the rights of minorities, especially in the arena of 'moral issues'.

At its most extreme, the conviction that differences cannot be reconciled within the larger framework casts the minority as a kind of social outlaw. Thus, the woman seeking to assert her (minority) rights is problematic, a process clearly demonstrated in the alienation of Irish women who have (legal) abortions. So outraged would the 'common good' be by the provision of abortion services in Ireland for the not inconsiderable number of Irish women requiring them, that these women have to travel abroad in secrecy and under legal threat to achieve their purposes.

In practice, personal liberty is predicated on social consensus; that is, we are permitted the limited exercise of personal rights dependent on the given social order. Equally, prevailing notions of the common good are ideologically constructed. The prevailing ideology in contemporary Ireland is composed of a patriarchal mixed-economy capitalism tempered by some social welfare provision.

The social consensus is constructed through a dialectic composed in part of ideas of monetarism mitigated by social justice; of a conservative catholic morality mitigated by pragmatic compassion.

In practise, this means that, while we agree that abortion should be illegal, we are disturbed that women in crisis might be forcibly restrained from seeking (lawful) abortion abroad. While we are unshakeable in our belief that the act of abortion is a grievous sin, we forgive, privately and in religious confession, the woman who has been driven to such an unfortunate action.

Now, any question of moral choice presupposes a number of factors:

* that a choice may be made between viable possibilities;

* that there is a protagonist to make that choice;
* that that protagonist has the authority to make the choice.

Where the issue of choice is raised by a pregnancy, these factors may be formulated thus:

* is there more than a single course of action which may be pursued?
* is the pregnant woman, the protagonist, to make the decision between such actions?
* does she have the moral right to do so?

There are also different kinds of choices which may be considered:

* *Pragmatic Choice*: where the choice is to be made simply for pragmatic, personally identified, reasons;
* *Altruistic Choice*: where the choice is to be made for idealistic or impersonally identified reasons;
* *Moral Choice*: a dialectic where the pragmatic is informed by the altruistic.

Every woman knows, and this knowledge would appear to be universal in time and culture, that any pregnant woman has a pragmatic choice: she may commit herself to the pregnancy or she may terminally interfere with its course. (She may also postpone the issue, hope for a miscarriage or abandon the resulting infant, practices known to continue in Ireland.)

Again pragmatically speaking, we know that pregnant women, as the 'holders of the baby', assume the role of protagonist in choice (although individual women may modify this role with regard to partner, family, friends etc).

The final question is more problematic as it raises the question of whether women may exercise a moral right to act as their own protagonists where issues of choice arise. Feminists proposing a moral agency in women develop this very question.

In her pioneering feminist work *The Second Sex*, published originally in the late 1940s and repeatedly banned in Ireland, Simone de Beauvoir explored the philosophical concept of woman as the 'other', a concept central to any discussion of the moral agency of women. To be 'other' implies exclusion from the norm; it is to be peripheral, marginal. Women, in de Beauvoir's analysis, are peripheral, marginal; the same women who make pragmatic decisions, decisions which surely have moral content and implications. The question now is: how are women, if we are truly 'other' (the condition of being female under patriarchy), to reconcile the pragmatic with the altruistic in a moral exercise? Mary Daly locates the question thus: 'Sexist society maintains its grasp on the psyche by keeping it divided against itself'.

This is simply the central contradiction, even the tragedy, of women's actual lives under patriarchy, and the source of women's overburdening guilt. That women shoulder this burden is the site of their courage, a courage rarely and insufficiently acknowledged in a culture where courage is measured in terms of men at war.

The rule of the fathers, Mary Daly's definition of patriarchy, regards moral exercise in women as not merely inappropriate, but impossible. The philosopher Schopenhauer described the state of women as 'moral infancy', while Otto Weininger wrote in 1906: 'A woman cannot grasp that one must act from principle; as she has no continuity she does not experience the necessity for logical support of her mental processes... she may be regarded as "logically insane".'

Women may be regarded as ordinary participants in society insofar as they possess such civil rights as the right to vote, to work, to own property, to initiate divorce proceedings (and it must be remembered that where women enjoy such rights, they have been achieved through the efforts of generations of feminist activism). These civil rights are, of course, the ordinary rights of citizens in western democracies, but they do not, alas, necessarily presuppose a moral agency or its exercise.

It may well be that these questions will be the divider between mainstream (civil rights) and radical (moral agency) feminism, with abortion as the focussing issue.

WOMEN'S MORALITY IN SOCIETY

[My] main object, the desire of exhibiting the misery of oppression, peculiar to women, that arises out of the partial laws and customs of society.
Mary Wollstonecraft, *The Wrongs of Woman*, 1798

Because the reproductive experience of individuals is such a private affair, we tend to think of such activity as being outside of the realm of law or social policy. However, population questions have, in the last two hundred years, become matters of public debate and government action. The decision to permit or prohibit the manufacture, distribution and advertising of contraceptive devices is, for example, a clear demonstration of public law involvement in citizens' private behaviour.

Equally, the existence and nature of abortion laws differ according to prevailing social policy - in China, for example, abortion is an integral part of the state reproductive policy; elsewhere, restricted access to abortion reflects a social commitment to population expansion. In Ireland, the existence of an anti-abortion law, bolstered by a constitutional guarantee of the right to life of the unborn, is an unambiguous statement of public policy, irrespective of the private practice of silent thousands of our 'criminal' citizens (women).

Such questions of social policy very often also raise the spectre of race survival. Dreadful experiments into human reproduction were carried out on persons of expendable race in Nazi concentration camps while abortion was denied to Aryan women, who were encouraged to breed a 'pure' race. Some Black male activists in the USA have argued against women's reproductive freedom, seeing contraception and abortion as tools of genocide. Similar fears have been expressed in regard to family planning programmes in the Third World. Meanwhile, wealthy right-wing organisations exhort white, middle-class French women to increase the size of their families; educated, middle-class women in Hong Kong are offered financial advantages to the family if they have children. In Ireland, the 'right to life' movement lobbies for subsidies for nuclear families (usually middle-class) at the expense of the single-parent unit (often working-class, certainly financially and socially disadvantaged).

Behind all of these initiatives lies a single, shared, premise: only certain people have the right to breed. And who decides? Not the individual woman - this is patriarchy, after all - but an assortment of outside agencies: the racist ideology, the right-wing pressure group, the authoritarian state. Behind the premise lies the same fear: if we don't breed enough, the hated others ('the yellow peril') will take us over. The American anti-abortionist, Fr Paul Marx, whose speciality is a pickled-foetus roadshow, neatly summarises this viewpoint thus: 'The white Western world is committing suicide through contraception and abortion' (Human Life Centre, Minneapolis, USA).

'[T]he preservation of life seems to be rather a slogan than a genuine goal of the anti-abortion force' writes Ursula K LeGuin. 'Control over behaviour; power over women. Women in the anti-choice movement want to share in male power over women and do so by denying their own womanhood, their own rights and responsibilities' *Dancing at the Edge of the World*, 1989.

If, as we have seen, individual actions take place within society, within ideology, the question of moral agency comes into focus when we encounter fundamental conflicts in the moral arena, as in the problematic area of maternal versus (proposed) foetal rights, where the social imperative is weighted against the woman. The greater the claim of the foetus (an entity which clearly cannot enter moral debate on its own behalf, a not inconsequential factor when personhood has been traditionally linked to the capacity for consciousness and decision), the more important the recognition of women's moral agency, of she who must bear the moral responsibility of her actions.

The so-called 'right to life' movement argues unambiguously that, while women may have a pragmatic choice of action in pregnancy, they have no right to moral agency; that is, that the foetus's claim self-evidently overwhelms any proposed moral agency in women. (Mary Daly adds that, according to this view, aborted foetuses are to be more mourned than adult human beings killed in war.)

In pregnancy, this struggle for control and responsibility is manifest in the issues which women confront, the 'hard' questions raised in non-directive pregnancy counselling:

* what are the viable options in your situation?
* how will you cope with your grief/anger/guilt? - whatever your decision
* how will you reconcile your decision with your conscience/god/religion?
* how would you feel after an abortion?

Social services correspondent Mary Maher writes:

> The phrase 'non-directive' has become fairly familiar as a description of that kind of therapeutic help which offers a client neither advice nor judgement, but a sympathetic ear ... [The] conviction is that people can make choices, good choices, for themselves, and have the right to do so, and that the therapist is there only to facilitate that process ... Basic assumptions from which client-centred therapy springs [are] ... that the individual is basically trustworthy, has the capacity and the right to make decisions about life, and the ability to establish a set of values ... Most important, they take responsibility for those choices, a necessary part of the growth process.
>
> *The Irish Times*, 20 November 1986

For Irish women choosing termination, and given our particular cultural heritage, moral exercise is located in the recognition of a prima facie right to life of the unborn which may only be overridden with justification, or good reason, to be provided by the pregnant woman herself.

Apart from surveys undertaken by Open Line Counselling, there has been little study of the abortion experience of Irish women, or of the reasons why Irish women choose abortion as an option in crisis pregnancy. Commenting on her decision to terminate her pregnancy, one Irish woman wrote: 'I would still like to think I can have a good life. I intend to go back and start anew and I don't regret my decision.' A common theme running through women's decision-making process concerning a crisis pregnancy is worry about how the pregnancy, if brought to term, would affect others, principally parents and existing children. Summarising the reasons given for considering abortion, Open Line Counselling reported as follows:

> Many younger women feel unprepared for a child, particularly where family and social support is unlikely or insufficient. Many women are also anxious to avoid causing hurt to their parents, especially where a parent has health problems. Older women are worried about the effects of another pregnancy on a grown family, and also about the possibility of a sub-normal child. Instability in the relationship with the putative father, whether casual acquaintance, ex-boyfriend, or where a marriage is under stress, is another common factor.
>
> Separated women with an extra-marital pregnancy are concerned about the irregular status of their relationship with the putative father and also about the threat to their separation agreements if the husband is unsympathetic to the pregnancy. Professional women are increasingly concerned about their future training and employment prospects, particularly in nursing and teaching. Most women decide to seek termination of pregnancy because of a multiplicity of these pressures. (October 1983)

While children born out of wedlock are no longer stigmatised in law as 'illegitimate', post-referendum Ireland has not been notable for its regard for its mothers. A number of tragic cases, from the death in childbirth of a 15 year old girl to the sacking of a teacher for giving birth to the child of a separated man, have come to light since the Human Life amendment of 1983. The lessons of these cases, and the social attitudes they reveal, are not lost on other women with unplanned pregnancies.

Although not all of these considerations will be foremost in a woman's mind when she is exploring her options in a crisis pregnancy, they help form the context in which her decisions must be made.

Furthermore, in a patriarchal society, there is the problem of the role of men in women's lives which is at best ambiguous, at worst, fatal.

In the social arena and mirroring women's domestic responsibilities, the so-called 'caring' professions are, at the helping level, almost exclusively staffed by women. Primary care is given by women; status and authority is male.

On a more sinister level, the European witchcraze of 1450-1750, described by Matilda Joslyn Gage in 1893 as 'the age of supreme despair for women', saw the slaughter by men of a minimum of 200,000 women. In the 1970s a new genre of pornography, depicting the real-life murder of women by men, 'snuff movies', brought the witchcraze to the domestic video screen. Men rape, murder, abandon, dominate, disenfranchise women.

Successful women, riding on the achievements of feminism, boast that they are 'just one of the boys', that women 'make dreadful bosses', that as a woman you have to be twice as good but so what? When was the last time a patently high achieving male boasted that he was 'just one of the girls'?

For all our delirious need to believe that men like us, respect us, treasure us, the evidence suggests to the contrary. 'He's just a woman', is a term of abuse, not of respect. And where there is no liking, no respect, there is instead fear and loathing; there is unlikely to be any acknowledgement of rights, of agency, certainly no espousal, no guarantee.

These considerations become acute when women are faced with a crisis pregnancy. By definition, women become pregnant only through congress with men (messenger doves notwithstanding). Men are present in pregnancy, even though one of the common factors in crisis pregnancy is the absence of a man. At its crudest level, this absence is manifest in the man who denies his contribution to the pregnancy: 'It's not mine'. On a manipulative level, it's the man who decides what is to be done: 'the obvious thing is for you to have an abortion (lover/husband); 'I've decided she's to have an abortion' (father).

At its most compassionate, it's the man who withdraws completely from the situation: 'It's her decision'. The problem with this last is that it may, although by no means always, mask a retreat from involvement, it may be a refusal to commit. It is often a position taken by men who are not married to the pregnant woman; husbands tend to have more emphatic opinions (as befits their role as patriarchs) and expect their opinion to prevail, even where these opinions are in conflict with their wives' convictions.

How a man reacts to a crisis pregnancy will have a direct effect on the woman's experience of the pregnancy as the circumstances from which the pregnancy arises are crucial to the woman's moral classification of it; women are most reluctant to carry to term the product of a rape and equally reluctant to abort the product of a loving relationship.

Even in their absence, men are present. Even in this most elemental of female spheres, men are still an inescapable consideration.

For this reason, and by way of the generosity of women in their moral inclusion of men, women are acutely vulnerable to exploitation and manipulation. Consider this exhortation from Fr Bernard Haring concerning women pregnant from rape:

> We must, however, try to motivate her to consider the child with love because of its subjective innocence, and to bear it in suffering through to birth, whereupon she may consider her enforced maternal obligation fulfilled, after which she would try to resume her life with the sanctity that she will undoubtedly have achieved through the great sacrifice and suffering.

This is most sophisticated cruelty. Compare it with this account from the life of the Irish saint, Brigid:

> A certain woman who had taken the vow of chastity fell, through youthful desire of pleasure, and her womb swelled with child. Brigid, exercising the most strength of her ineffable faith, blessed her, caused the foetus to disappear, without coming to birth, and without pain. She faithfully returned the woman to health and to penance.
>
> Liam de Paor, *The Life of St. Brigid by Cogitatus* c. 650, (trans.) (unpub.)

Fathers of foetuses are now legally permitted (to at least attempt) to stop women from having abortions, or to insist on caesarian deliveries. Men are in a position to threaten women with withdrawal of material and emotional support if the woman does not abort a pregnancy which is unwanted by the man. These are positions of great power: personal, social, political. In the patriarchy, these positions are continually open to unchecked abuse.

TOWARDS A FEMINIST MORALITY OF CHOICE

She knows that masculine morality as it concerns her, is a vast hoax.

Simone de Beauvoir, *The Second Sex*, 1949

Feminism is not merely an issue but rather a mode of being.

Mary Daly, *Beyond God the Father*, 1973

Feminist philosophy proceeds from the proposition that women are valuable in and of ourselves, a proposition not found in patriarchal philosophy, religion or morality, which teach of the role and duty of women as relative to the absolute value of the man, the patriarch. 'Morally insane' (Weininger), women may be permitted certain courses of action, even in fertility, but only under the direction of male authority; thus, abortion laws, liberal or prohibitive, which remove the moral imperative from women.

Feminist morality restores this imperative. Where liberal philosophers and theologians argue for abortion within the patriarchal framework, feminism resists the scapegoating of women as victims (victims are not authors of moral behaviour). Women's experience, we argue, has an objective moral value.

Patriarchal 'morality' is hierarchical; only the dominant are valid originators of moral claims. Feminism is about no less than the de-structuring of this moral imperialism.

That I can think more clearly about [my abortion] now, and talk, and write about it, is entirely due to the moral courage and strength of women and men who have been working these thirty years for the rights and dignity and freedom of women, including the right to abortion.

Ursula K LeGuin, 1989

Contemporary feminism, as we have seen, has developed a unique system of 'self-help' networks and whereas 'self-help' is a process common to oppressed peoples, for feminism, the personal is political and 'self-help' is no less than the conscious response to women's perceived and stated needs; that is, a political intervention into patriarchal society on behalf of women, not only as individuals, but as a class. This response is possible only when based on listening - to ourselves and to other women. For feminism, this intervention is more than political - it is a moral commitment. Respect for women is a central dimension of this commitment; that is, a respect which acknowledges and celebrates moral agency in women.

The opposition to non-directive pregnancy counselling and the threats to other woman-centred services and activities are ideological and rooted in patriarchal philosophy. Evidence suggests they will become even more violent.

Ireland is unusual, although the present legal climate is certainly volatile, in that Irish women have not, in recent times, been jailed for seeking abortion or for helping women to procure abortions (potentially criminal activities under the law). Not that we congratulate ourselves on this record. Women all over the world have been brave enough to risk jail and worse on behalf of their sisters. And, where feminists in the 1970s provided humorous media fodder, proponents of choice in the 1980s are unemployable. Where students in the 1960s were 'revolting', contemporary student publications are the subject of protracted litigation.

The proposition that women have the right to choose does not enjoy favour as Ireland prepares for the federal Europe of the 1990s (where, to the embarrassment of the State, a Court of Human Rights application on these issues will have to be answered, together with a European Court of Justice reference). Equally, a campaign for abortion rights would certainly encounter opposition even from those women who currently seek (lawful) abortion services in Britain. Ten years ago, feminists had the opportunity to campaign - and a gallant bunch did - for the decriminalisation of abortion. Today, a referendum to remove Article 40.3.3 would have to be successful before the issue could be meaningfully raised.

If, as veteran Irish campaigner Mary Gordon contends: 'A measure of the strength of the feminist movement in any country is the strength and confidence of its abortion rights lobby', a challenge has been issued to the Irish Women's Movement. Now that we have a clearer idea, albeit with the wisdom of hindsight, where the ideological lines are drawn, it is a challenge which we will confront with the greatest urgency.

REFERENCES AND FURTHER READING

Arditti, Rita, Renate Duelli Klein and Shelley Minden (eds). *Test-tube Women: What Future for Motherhood?* London: Pandora Press, 1984

Caputi, Jane. *The Age Of The Sex Crime* London: The Women's Press, 1988

Daly, Mary. *Beyond God The Father* (1973) London: The Women's Press, 1986

Greer, Germaine. *The Madwoman's Underclothes* London: Picador, 1986

Greer, Germaine. *Sex and Destiny: The Politics of Human Fertility* London: Secker and Warburg, 1984

Greer, Germaine. *The Female Eunuch* London: Paladin, 1975

Le Guin, Ursula. *Dancing on the Edge of the World* New York: Grove Press, 1989

Moller Okin, Susan. *Women in Western Political Thought* London: Virago, 1980

Purcell, Betty. Interview with Mary Robinson and Mary McAleese *The Crane Bag* Vol 4 no 1, 1980

Riddick, Ruth. *Making Choices: The Abortion Experience of Irish Women* Dublin: Open Line Counselling, 1988

Spender, Dale. *Mothers of the Novel* London: Pandora Press, 1986